WE
THE PEOPLE
POWER

TINA WILSON

Copyright © 2022 by Tina Wilson.

ISBN 978-1-64133-879-0 (softcover)
ISBN 978-1-64133-880-6 (ebook)

All rights reserved. No part of this book may be reproduced or transmitted in any form or by any means, electronic or mechanical, including photocopying, recording, or by any information storage and retrieval system without express written permission from the author, except in the case of brief quotations embodied in critical reviews and certain other noncommercial uses permitted by copyright law.

Printed in the United States of America.

Brilliant Books Literary
137 Forest Park Lane Thomasville
North Carolina 27360 USA

WE THE PEOPLE POWER

The Great Tomorrows, Whispers Of Delight.
When We Empower, Freedoms Right.
The Great Tomorrows, Whispers Of Faith.
4 Loves Rights, & Seeking Safe.

The Great Tomorrows, Whispers Of Anew.
Shimmering Rays, 4 Peaceful Dew.
The Great Tomorrows, A Man's Dream.
Awes Uplifting Effect, In Every Stream.

The Great Tomorrows, Paths Of Right.
4 Labors Of Love, Shining Bright.
The Great Tomorrows, Whispers Of Grace.
4 Goals Of Peace, 4 Loves Embrace.

The Great Tomorrows, Whispers Of Awe.
4 Leaders Uniting, & Peaceful Law.
The Great Tomorrows, Whispers 2 Revive.
Compassion In Mans Heart, 4 Love 2 Thrive.

The Great Tomorrows, Whispers Of Reason.
4 Peace On Earth, In Social Season.

Great Peacemakers R A Gem.
4 Humbleness, From Within.
Roots 4 All, Human Rights.
4 Legacies Of Loves Delights.

Within The Heart, Of Every Him.
Great Peacemakers, R A Gem.
4 Love 2 Thrive & Really Flow..
4 Peace On Earth, 2 Root & Grow.

Compassions Rights, 4 All 2 See.
4 The Betterment Of Humanity.
Actions 4 Loves Peaceful Rights.
4 World Of Bliss & Delights.

Great Peacemakers 4 Love In Law.
4 Whispers Of, Heavens Call.
Lift & Lead, With Heart & Mind.
4 Worlds Of Joy, Just & Kind.

4 All 2 Thrive In Love, Sown.
Peacemakers, Must Be, Known.

A Mother's Eyes, Just 4 Me,
Seeds Of Joy, Our Family, Tree.
Little Links Of Love, So Pure.
4 Our Legacies, 2 Endure.
A Mother's Eyes, Just 4 Me,
Daddy's 2, Our Future, Tree.
Little Eyes, & A Little Nose.
As Our Hearts, Really, Froze.

Into A World, Amazing & Anew.
Welcoming, Our Little, Crew..
Aunties, Nose, & Grandpas, Ears.
At First, We Had Some, Fears.
Of How 2 Hold Learning 2 Share.
Links Of Loves, Loyal, Layer..
Oh So Small, Yet Such, A Force.
A Mother's Eyes, A New, Course.

Of Feeding, Changing & A Laugh.
A Little, Babe, Changed Our Path.
Now A Mama Bear, Full, Of Light.
Gazing At, Our Child At Night.
We Shall Be There In A Blink.
Our Little Child, Precious, Link.
Teaching Us, As Years, Go Past.
A Mother's, Love Always, Last.

Even When, We Leave This Place.
Or Love Remains, Thru Time & Space.
Angel Eyes, & Shimmering, Sounds.
Feel Our Love Upon Life's, Grounds ?
Forever, There Our Joy, Remains.
Within A Child's Tiny, Grains.
May U Grow, 2 Be A Loving Light.
Our Little Child, Of Joy & Delight !

I Saw A Shimmer, Light, Up The Sky.
As, I, Witnessed, An Angel, Passing, By.
Rainbows Danced, Upon Her, Wings.
Within My Soul, The Memory, Sings.

Splashes, Of Sunlight, Drifted, Thru.
Glorious Wings, Of Twinkling, Dew..
Surrounded By, A Shimmering, Grace.
Within A Angels, Loving, Embrace.

Her Face Glowed, With, A Radiant, Bliss.
Within, The, Shimmers, Of A Angels, Kiss !

Let Not Doubt, Get In Life's, Way.
Of Creating, Miracles Everyday.
Be Them Big Or A Merry, Mini.
Create Miracles, 4 Joy Of Plenty.

Be It Smile Or A Loving Kind Word.
Let Them Flow, 4 Love That's Heard.
Witnessed 2, In Tears Of Love & Joy.
When Miracles In Action, We Deploy.

Also Known, As Love, Vibrant & Alive.
In Merry Miracles, Souls Do Thrive.
Within The Flow Of Love, That Inspires.
Miracles Live Within, Joyous Attires.

Have Some Goals, A Vision A Dream.
2 Create, Merry Miracles In Life's Stream.
Tis Easy 2 Witness, Angels Eyes Flicker.
As Love Resides, In Compassions Clicker.

Then Miracles Bloom 2 Be, 4 Ever Known.
Where Seeds Of Love, Are Sown & Grown !

The Power Of Words & A Good Speech.
Can Empower, Loves Rights 2 Teach.
Like Sojourner, Dr. King, Words Of Right.
That Echo 4 Centuries, Of Peace & Light.

The Power Of Words, Useless, Is Rage.
Better 2 Ignite Sparks, 4 Loves Stage.
Use Not Fist, Fire, Nor Bullets, Or Wars.
Tis Words, That Can Open, Loves Doors.

Knocking Hate Down, Making It Think.
The Power Of Words, 4 Love 2 Link.
Much Can Be Done, A Stroke Of A Pen.
4 Thoughts That Inspire, Peace 2 Win.

The Power Of Words, 4 Loves Rebirth.
Can Create Joyous, Heaven On Earth.
Use Words With Honor, Joy & Respect.
The Power Of Words, 4 Love 2 Protect.

Words Can Unite, 4 Real Peacemaking.
Ones Of Grace, 4 Loves Awakening.
Better 2 Battle, With The Heart & Mind.
4 A World Of Love, Not Morally Blind.

The Power Of Words, Beacons Of Light.
Can Inspire Worlds, Of Joyous Delight !

Police Into Peacemakers, What's It Take?
Freedom Of Choices, In Our Wake.
Police Into Peacemakers, Why Is It A Need?
4 Love In Action, 2 Fund & Feed.

Police Into Peacemakers, How Do Most Feel?
About Careers Of Cheers, 4 Love, That's Surreal?
Police Into Peacemakers, How Do We Protect?
We Take Actions 2 Inspire, Not Add 2 Neglect.

Police Into Peacemakers, Can We Act & Evolve?
4 Freedoms Rights Empowered, & Love 2 Resolve?
Police Into Peacemakers, What's The Effect, On You?
Being Forced 2 Tell Others, What They Can & Can't Do.

Police Into Peacemakers, Can Politicians, Uplift & Be?
Defenders Of Freedom Rights, 4 Social Honor, Set Free?
Police Into Peacemakers, Is Real Justice Alive & Well?
What's It Like 2 Evict Families, In Our Homeless Swell?

Police Into Peacemakers, What's It Feel Like, 2 Pretend?
That As A Nation, We Have Evolved, In More Rules Wind?
Police Into Peacemakers, Do U Act, 4 Others, 2 Heal?
Where Injustice Has Been Ignored, 4 Happy Honor, 2 Feel?

Police Into Peacemakers, Can U Unite, Respect & Evolve?
4 Whispers Of Heaven, 2 Root, Reign & Resolve?
Police Into Peacemakers, Do U Hire Those, In Real Need?
Citizens From Within That Town, 4 Honor In Actions, Feed?

Police Into Peacemakers, Do U Act 4 Freedom Of Choices, Rights ?
Then Take Actions Of Kindness, 4 Legacies Of Loves, Delights.
Police Into Peacemakers, What's It Like 2 Kick In, Others Doors ?
Do U Have Flashbacks Of Fear & Fright, From Our Drug Wars ?

Police Into Peacemakers, Can U Evolve & Step Up 2 The Plate ?
To Honor Freedoms Rights, 4 Love In Actions, Trait ?

Whispers Of Heaven, Many Don't Believe.
On Earth As In Heaven We All Can Achieve.
Thru Belief & Actions, 4 The World 2 Shine.
4 Whispers Of Heaven, 2 Thrive So Divine.

Whispers Of Heaven, 4 Eternal Joyous Ways.
Happens When All Play A Role, 2 End The Haze.
The Blocks The Goodness, 4 Heaven That's Fine.
In A World That Adds Actions, Oh So, Divine.

Without Man Made Suffering, Not Getting Along.
Within His Soul ,He Has The Power, 2 Create Strong.
Whispers Of Heaven, Eternal Echoes Of Loves Wake.
Are Created When, Loves Rights R Share, 4 Intake.

Whispers Of Heaven, 4 Merry Memories, That Thrive.
All It Takes Is Actions, That Keep, Kindness Alive.
4 All 2 Partake In Whispers Of Heavens, Real Rights.
Man Must Empower, 4 Worlds Of Awesome, Delights.

The Power Of Love, Is Meant, 2 Be Used.
Without It, Kindness, Can Not, Be, Fused.
The Power Of Love, Can End, Poverty & Wars.
4 Love In The Waves, Seas, Sands & Shores.

The Power Of Love, Is A, Miraculous, Force.
4 Heaven On Earth, & Hates, Divorce.
The Power Of Love, Is A Global & Social, Need.
4 Peace On Earth, 2 Spread, & Succeed.

The Power Of Love, Is Meant, 2 Be, Shared.
4 Compassion 2 Thrive, & Joy, Well Layered.
The Power Of Love, Should Not, Be Forsaken.
4 Heaven, On Earth, 2 Arise, & Awaken !

May Heavens Light, Fill Every Room.
4 Peace On Earth, To Bud & Bloom.
May Sharing Faith & Land Be Cool.
4 Peace On Earth, 2 Reign & Rule.

May Heavens, Wake, Fill The Air.
4 Worlds Of Awe, Just & Fair.
May All Men Use Hearts & Mind.
4 Peace On Earth, 2 All Mankind.

May Unity Thrive, 4 Goals Of Glory.
4 Peace On Earth, In All, Our Story.
May Men Get Long, 4 Loves Right.
4 Peace On Earth, 2 Take Flight.

I Had, A Dream, That, Man, Did, See,
That What's, Important, Is His Legacy.
Did He Stand 4 Peace & Freedom Of Choices,
Or Did He Oppress, All The, Silent Voices ?

Did He Empower & Uplift, The Socially, Broken,
Or Did He Share & Rejoice, 4 Glories, Token ?
I Had A Dream, He Quit, Bossing, All, Round,
& Within, His Weary, Soul, Love, Was Found.

When He Unites Kin, Forced, Way, Way, Apart.
Then, We Know He's Began, A Brand New, Start.

I Had A Dream, Man Took , Actions, 2 Get Along.
4 Heaven On Earth, 2 Grow, Vibrant & Strong.
I Had A Dream, Of Zero, Bad, Tactics, Galore.
4 Freedom Of Choices, Upon, Every, Shore !

Where Freedoms Rights, Light The Path.
All Achieve, On Loves Behalf.
Where Freedoms Rights, Rein & Rule.
Success Flows, 4 Liberties, Tool.

Where Freedom Grows, All Act 2 Evolve.
4 Liberties, Path, 2 Resolve.
Where Freedoms Known, All Do Thrive.
4 Love In Action, That's Alive.

Where Freedom Stands, 4 Production.
There R Not Paths, Of Corruption
Where Freedom Lives & Walks The Earth.
All Are Treated, With Much Worth.

All Are Born, With Freedoms Rights.
Unless Man Binds, Liberties Lights.
Freedom 2 Achieve, Honorable Success.
Lights The Way, 4 Loves, Progress.

4 Careers Of Cheers, So All Can Explore.
Freedom Rights, Shall Endure.
Where Freedom Is, One Can Tell.
All R Treated, Fine & Swell.

Where Freedom Is, None R Socially Bound.
So Love Lives On, 4 Success, Aground.
Freedom All Need, 2 Seek Share & Explore.
Take Freedoms Rights Away, Adds 2 Poor.

Where Freedom Reins, All Do, Thrive.
Keeping The Powers, Of Love Alive.
Take Freedoms Away, Civil Unrest Grows.
From Lack Of Choices, In Life's, Flows.

Millions Write & Fight, 4 Freedoms 2 Achieve.
Yet Some Learned Not, Love Rights, 2 Believe.
Freedom Is A Power, All Should, Set Free.
4 Whispers Of Heavens, Now Legacy.

Where Freedoms Rights, Light The Way.
Pure Love, Lives On, Everyday.
Man That Binds,Freedoms Path 2 Thrive.
Has Yet, 2 Learn Honor, 4 Love Alive.

Where Freedom Does Light, The Path.
All Achieve, On Loves Behalf.
Where Freedom, Lives, There R Choices.
4 Whispers Of Heavens, Now Rejoices.

How Does Charity, Keep Govs Mind Socially Broke ?
They Learn Not To Give Needs, For Taxes, In Honors Yoke.
Tears Of Joy Are Not Witnessed, Nor Angel Eyes Seen.
Charity Keeps Us All Poor, Lacking Successes, Scene.

To Empower Your Gov & People Is Better, Love On The Spot.
When We Give We Receive, Merry Memories, Not Forgot.
All Govs Must Learn Proper To Teach Others, To Empower.
Charity Is All About Tax Breaks, Not Freedoms, To Flower.

Tis Our Obligation To Teach Proper, Honor In, Earns Right.
For All To Have Paths Of Success, Not Fines & Fees Of Fright.
When We Enable Govs, We Are Not Doing, Any Good, At All.
Tis Vital All Meet Honor In Actions, Good Great, Social Call.

For Tax To Relax, Careers Of Cheers, When We Teach For Love.
We Play A Small Role, In Creating Heaven On Earth, As Above.
When We Ignore Injustice, Corruptions, None Really, Learn.
How Vital It Is To Meet Honor In Funds, For Merry Morals In Earn.

Charities & Foundations, Can Be A Bonus, When They Explore.
What Freedom Really Is, Choices To Seek, Learn & Endure.
When We Teach Proper, Honor In Funds, For A Good Social Pal.
We Can Create, Heaven Upon Earth, Here & Now.

The Powers, Of Loves Delight.
Awakens Peace , In Flight.
The Powers Of Humble, Unity.
Empowers Ways, Of Immunity.

The Powers, Of Sharing, Spaces.
Can End, All Homeless Traces.
The Powers Of Love, So Grand.
Allows Peace On Earth, 2 Stand.

The Powers Of Good, Evolutions.
Shall End All, Prides Pollutions.
The Powers Of Peacemaking Right.
Create Worlds, Of Joys Delight.

The Powers Of Freedom Of Choices.
Fir Liberty In Actions, Now Rejoices.
The Powers Of Leaders Uniting.
Shall End The Ways Of Fighting.

The Powers Of Compassions Right.
Shall End The Ways, Of Fright.
The Powers Of Love & Grace.
Create Peace On Earths, Embrace !

War Is, A Social, Addiction,
From Pride & Egos, Affliction.
We Must Not, Add To Neglect,
For Peace On Earth, To Protect.

For Angel Eyes, On The Spot.
For Kindness, Not Forgot.
For Compassion, To Freely, Grow.
Within Loves, Eternal Flow.

For Heaven On Earth, In A Blink.
Man Must Use His Heart, To Link.
Actions, That Fund & Empower.
Freedom Of Choices, To Flower.

Many Have, Given With Glee.
To Uplift, Freedoms, Legacy.
When We Invest In, All's Success.
Miracles Thrive, For Love, To Bless !

Floetry Flows, From The Spirit & Soul.
Whispers Of Heaven, 4 Love As A Whole.
Floetry Is Of Truth, 4 Grace, Awe & Joy.
Whispers Of Angels, 4 Truth , 2 Deploy,

Floetry Revives Spirits, Socially, Broken.
Whispers Of Healing, 4 Words, Not Spoken.
Floetry Just Flows, Within Wisdoms Wake.
Whispers Of Compassion, In Loves Intake.

Floetry Is Flowing Words Of Wisdom, Known.
Whispers Of Kindness, 4 Love In Action Grown.
Floetry Is Living Words Of Truth, In Lifes Cup.
Whispers Of Sharing Faith, Soul Food, 4 Up.

Floetry Is Uplifting, A Great Global Need.
Whispers Of Unity, 4 Loves Fruitful Feed.
Floetry Is 4 Peace, Spirits & Souls, Anew.
Whispers Of Laughter, Love, Pure & True.

Floetry Is Euphoric, 4 Joyous Boost, Of Awe.
4 Whispers Of Heaven, When Love Comes 2 Call.
Floetry Is A Gift, 4 Teaching, What's Proper & Right.
Whispers Of Tomorrow, 4 Peace On Earths, Delight.

I Saw My Reflection, Upon The Moon.
& Knew That I 'd Be Leaving Soon.
Amazed I Was, As My Wingspan Grew.
How Dancing Rainbows Shimmered Thru.

My Crippled Body In Pain, No More.
Or Tossed Out Another Door.
As Stardust Lights, Twinkled Anew.
Up I Drifted, As My Wingspan Grew.

Giving Thanks 2 God, 4 Letting Me Go.
Back 2 Where, All Truths A Glow.
My Soul Rejoiced My Spirit Within.
& As A Small Child , I Began Again.

Lots Thought They'd Have A Chance.
Yet Failed To Notice, Moms Last Dance.
Rejoice In Gods Will, 2 Start A New.
& Know My Love Is, 4 Ever True.

See The Twinkles, In Their Eye.
& Know It's Grandma, Drifting By.
& In The Clouds & Fragrant Smell.
My Love Remains, In Memories Swell.

Know I Gave, All The Love I Had.
Reflect In The Moments & Be Glad.
There's Lots Of Rooms, 2 Enjoy 4 Free.
In The Depths Of Pure Love & Eternity !

Elections Can Be, Of Freedoms Flicker.
Unless They Add, 2 More Social Bicker.
Every Few Years, They Return 2 Fight.
Keeping Unity Off Track, 4 Loves Light.

Funds Given, Bribery, Is The Now Course.
Taking Honor Away, 4 Dignities, Force.
Most Write Of Interference, From Others.
Not Seeking 2 Learn Of Unity, 4 Brothers.

Terms 2 Short, Ones There 4 Every Town.
Where Nothing Good, Really Goes Down.
Experience Matters, Changing All The Time.
Keeps Stability At Bay, 4 Freedoms, Chime.

Our Laws Are 2 Many 2 Even Count, 4 Sure.
Yet Zero Speak Of That 4 Freedom 2 Endure.
Elections, Could Be Great, If Gone The Greed.
4 Labors Of Love, That Are A Social Need.

Now If They All Worked Together 4 Good Goals.
Then Freedoms Rights Could Be, 4 Happy Souls.
Other Nations Are Blamed, Yet Right Here Within.
Is Where Their Loyalty Starts, 4 Freedom, 2 Begin.

I Am, A Gem, A Ruby, A Twinkling Light, In The Dark.
A Part Of Your Very Soul, 4 Joyous Loves, Social, Spark.
I Am Vital, 2 A Society, 4 Foundations, Of Honors, Effect.
With God Given, Birth Rights, 2 Be Treated, With Respect..

I Am, Women Of Wisdom, Raining Knowledge Joy & Grace.
4 Legacies, Of Love, 2 Echo, On, Thru Out, All Time & Space.
Many Times I Go Without, From Lots Of Mans, Proud, Choices.
As He Suppresses, Our Roles, In Society, 4 Love, Of Rejoices.

I Am The Womb, Of Life, The Shero At Times, Never, Heard.
From Mans Teachings, That Exclude, Us, Rules Of Absurd.
My Soul Shimmers & Shines, When Man, Takes Time, 2 See.
The Vital Role I Play, In Empowering, Love In Actions, Legacy.

Not All Men, Suppress, Of Course, But Most See Really, Not.
The Vital Roles, We Play, When Loves, Been, Socially, 4 Got.
There's Wars, Neglect, Very Little, Compassion, Active & Alive.
I Am A Women, On A Mission, 4 Love, 2 Blossom & Daily Thrive.

I Have Important Herstorys, Of Miracles Not Yet, Really, Known.
Where Seeds Of Pride, Carry On, From Love, Not, Socially, Sown.
My Role, Is Often Blocked By Men, Whom Lack, Honor & Respect.
4 Ending Our World, Of Hate, 4 Love In Action, 2 Prosper & Protect.

I Am A Women,Of Multitudes & Millions Just Waiting, 2 Really, See.
When Mans, Going 2 Step Up & Invest In, Love In Actions, Legacy..
4 Freedom Of Choices, Careers Of Cheers, Broken Spirits, No More
4 The Powers Of Love, & Peace On Earth 2 Endure !

I Am A Dad, A Parent Needed, For Good Uplifting, Evolutions.
For A Society, To Be Secure, For Futures, Of Great Solutions.
My Role Is Slighted, For At Home Needs, To Exhausted & Tired.
We Usually Pass Over First, Lack Of Real Healthcare Hired.

For Taxes, Paid Total Healthcare, With Choices That, Represent.
My Tax Funds R Spent Properly, 4 Freedom, Of Our, Betterment.
The "Cats In The Cradle," Much Spoken, In A Song, Of The Heart.
I Have Personally Witnessed My Friends, Not Get, A Good, Start.

Crippling From Repetitive Motions, Obesity, From Lack Of Change.
Most Study Not What's Important, In Company's & That's, Strange.
Hurtful 2 Our Nation, Millions Lost On The Streets Of Rage, Man Made.
From Lack Of Freedom & Opportunities, For Multi Funds, Upgrade.

On Some Streets, All The Dads, Are Incarcerated, Spirits Now, Dead.
From Man Made Laws The Suppress, Our Freedom Of Choices, Fed.
As The Dads Faces, R Posted, 4 All The Town Folk, 2 Witness & See.
They Had Not Choices, For Income, All Of That, Drains Our, Society.

For Those Who Fought 4 Freedom A Broad, While Loosing, It At Home.
War Wounds, Generations, 4 Ever, More Neglected, Forced, To Roam.
While McMansions, Are The New Fad, The Homegrown, R Daily, Tossed.
Our Gov, Is 2 Be Our Boulder Our Rock 4 Moral Lines, Not Crossed.

When Society's Value The People & Clear Daily Routes, 2 Empower.
Love In Action, Can Actually Bloom, 4 Freedom Of Choices, 2 Flower.
Tax 2 Relax, Total Healthcare, Please Take Off, Your Blinders, 2 See.
What Matters Most, Is Ones Soul, 4 Echoes Of Loves, Joyous, Legacy.

    Let, Joy, Awaken Spirit & Soul.
    4 Merry, Memories, As A Whole.
    Let, Faith, Sparkle Oh So, Shine.
    Sharing Faith Is Love, Divine.

    Let Love, Guide Light, Life's, Path.
    Add, Happy, Humor On Joys, Behalf.
    Let Humbleness Be, A Moral Course.
    4 Love In Actions Awesome, Force.

    Let Fear, Not, Bind U, In Any Way.
    Set Goals, 4 Passion Everyday.
    Invest In Paths, 4 Peace, On Earth.
    Rejoice In Loves, Loyal, Rebirth.

    Let Others, Shine, 2 Share & Evolve.
    Welcome Peace, 4 Love 2 Resolve.
    Uplift, Freedoms, Beacon Of Light.
    4 Love In Actions, Joyous, Sight.

Let Your Spirit, Fly At Rest, Or Awake.
Never Neglect, Pure, Loves Intake.
Let Wisdom, Be Known, Freedoms Right.
With Respect & Honor 4 Loves, Invite..

Let Peace On Earth Be Your, Legacies.
Within Echoes Of Loves Eternal, Breeze.
Invite Others Along 4 Life's, Amazing, Ride.
Within The Gentle Seas Of 4 Evers, Tide !

I Woke Up, With Wings, 2 My Joyous, Delight.
As My Body Faded, My Spirit, Took Flight.
I Witnessed, Tears Of Sorrow, Down On Earth.
Reflections, Of Memories, & Loves Rebirth.

As I Tried, 2 Let Them Know, I Am Still Here.
I Could Not Get Past, Their, Sadness & Fear.
I Fluttered Around, Tucked Them, In Bed.
Whispers In The Wind, Of Love Still Fed.

I Asked Other Angels, What Do I Do ?
They Said Keep Trying, 4 Love, That's True.
I Knocked Over Things, Changed The Station.
2 Play Our Songs, Out Of Loves Obligation.

I Fluttered By, 4 Them 2 Smell, My Perfume.
Waiting Patiently, 4 Their Faith, 2 Bloom.
Our Society Teaches, Death Is The End.
So It Was Challenge, In Loves, Joyous, Wind.

I Entered Their Dreams, 2 Let Them Know.
Mom's Still Around, In Loves, Eternal Flow.
One Day They Were Discussing , Old Memories.
& Both Realized, I Was Still, In Loves Breeze.

When They Started Comparing, Little Events.
Be It Our Songs, Or Moms, Fragrant Scents.
They Understood Now, I Was In, Their Lives.
Where The Bond, Of Love, Flows & Survives.

No Longer Were They Sad, Just By Knowing.
The Spirit Lives On, & Continues, Flowing.
My Mission Complete, In Memories, Of Delight.
I Spread My Wings & Took Joyous Flight !

May All, Leaders, Be Led, By The Heart.
4 Peace, On Earth, 2 Get, A, Great, Start.
May All, Leaders, Take Actions, Of Good.
2 Be Led, By Love, As, They, Should.

May All Leaders, Stop & Think, Twice.
About Joyous, Love, 4 Daily, Sacrifice.
May All, Leaders, Step Up, 2 Life's, Plate.
& End The Neglect, Caused, By Hate.

May All, Leaders, Unite, 4, A, Good, Cause.
& Let Go Of, Pride, Instead, Of Adding, Walls.
May All, Leaders, Spread, Joy & Good, News.
Instead, Of Adding, Another, Social, Bruise.

May All, Leaders, Uplift, Those, Slighted.
4 Peace On Earth, Empowered & Invited.
May All, Leaders, Sow, Of Good, Thinking.
4 Love, In Action, That's, Socially, Linking.

May All, Leaders, Be, Kind, Of, Course.
4 Peace On Earths, Joyous, Force.
May All Leaders, Act, 4 Unity, Alive.
4 Heaven On Earth, 2 Prosper & Thrive !

I Saw The World, As It, Should Be.
Without War, Oppression Or Poverty.
Where All Were Welcomed & Invited.
& None Were, Purposely, Slighted.

Where Opportunities Arose, In A Blink.
& All Were Treated, As A Needed, Link.
Where There Was No Rape Or Incarceration.
& All Were Welcomed, With, Inspiration.

Where Gov's, Gave In Return, 4 Taxes Paid.
& None Were Exploited, In Egos, Shade.
Where All Were Welcomed, With Joy & Glee..
& There Was No Hate, As Love, Was Set Free.

I Saw A World, Where Love, Was Found.
& By Poverty, None, Were Bound.
I Saw The Men, Actually Get Along.
4 Peace On Earth, 2 Grow Strong !

Having A Goal,
Feeds The Soul.
4 All Progress,
Is Real, Success.

If Just, 4 Wealth,
Selfish, Stealth.
4 All, Betterment.
Moments, Well Spent.

Return, Good Deeds.
4 Soulful, Needs.
4 Peace & Grace,
& Loves, Embrace !

The Power, Of Love & Loyalty.
Is What, Creates Our Destiny.
By Linking, Life, & Holding Hands.
Love Is Fed, From Seas, 2 Sands.

Echoes Of, Moments In Time.
Within Memory's, Loving Chime.
Be It Adults, Or A Small, Child.
Memories, Where Love Grows Wild.

In Old Age, Some, Fade Away.
Yet Remain, In, Memory's Clay.
Linking Love, & Our Dreams.
Within Echoes, Of Living Streams.

Friends, R A Need, In Our Lives.
So Love Lives & Survives.
If They Step Back, 4 Separations
Know, They Have Obligations.

As Some Shall Part, In Our Mist.
We Have The Memories, 2 Enlist.

In The Valleys Of Delight, Theres Compassion.
Actions On The Spot, None Do Ration.
In The Valleys Of Delight, There's Teaching.
Instructions Of Productions, Far Reaching.

In The Valleys Of Delight, There's Not Fees.
Where Giving, Lives On In Life's, Breeze
In The Valleys Of Delight, There's Grace
4 All Empowered, 4 Loves, Daily Embrace.

In The Valleys Of Delight, There's Evolutions
Where Peace Exist, 4 Pure Loves, Solutions.
In The Valleys Of Delight, All Are Included.
4 Love In Action, That's Socially Saluted.

In The Valleys Of Delight, There's Peace On Earth.
Where All R Vital Links, 4 A Glorious, Rebirth.
In The Valleys Of Delight, Wisdom Is Shared.
In Merry Memories, 4 Loyal Love, Layered.

In The Valleys Of Delight, Sharing Faith Exist.
Where All R Welcomed, 2 Be Angels In Our Mist.
In The Valleys, Of Delight, Kinships, Are United.
4 Heaven On Earth, That's Socially Invited.

In The Valleys Of Delight, Respect & Kindness Meet.
4 All Successful Paths, & Poverties, 2 Defeat.
In The Valleys Of Delight, None R Extorted.
4 Happy Honor In Funds, 4 Love, Imported.

In The Valleys, Of Delight, Gov's Give In Return.
4 Happy Honor, In Knowing, Love, With All Earn.
In The Valleys Of Delight, 5% Taxes, Are Paid.
4 The Peoples Security, Of Successes, Upgrade.

In The Valleys Of Delight, There's Not Bickering.
4 Peace On Earth, That's Alive & Flickering.

May These Words Assist,
Belief In Angels In Our Mist.

As My Rebirth Begins,My Body, Fades.
Within The Seas Of Loves Upgrades.
My Shimmering Wings Hidden Within.
As My Spirit Arises ,4 Love On A Spin.

At Times I Have Minutes ,Others, Years.
4 Good Fruits In Action & Happy Cheers.
I'm Letting Go, Now, Yet 4 Ever I Still, Exist.
Within Loves Rain, As A Angel In The Mist.

As I Fly Free, In The Seas, Of Delight.
My Love Remains, In Memories Of Light.
Mourn Not Distance, Just Joyously Reflect.
On Merry Memories Loyal, Loves, Effect.

Be Thankful 4 The Happiness, We Had.
I'm No Longer Suffering, Please, Be Glad
Waste Not, Precious Moments In, Any, Fear.
4 My Love Remains Always, Present & Near.

Close Your Eyes & Feel A Joyous, Legacy.
Within Echoes Of Loves, Amazing, Memory.
Rejoice, With Those, That, Walk This Earth.
& Me Go, 2 Enjoy Loves, Joyous, Rebirth !

Whispers From A Poetess.
4 Love & Happy Bliss.
4 Worlds Of Awe & Of Joy.
4 Love In Action 2 Deploy.

Whispers Of A Elders, Soul.
4 Happy Hope As A Whole.
Sharing Faiths Silly Sprinkle.
4 Peace On Earth 2 Twinkle.

Whispers Of Laughing, Love.
4 Peace On Earth As Above.
Worlds Of Awe Dancing Dreams.
Freedoms Rights Silly Streams.

Whispers Of Love & Laugh.
4 Peace On Earth Joys Behalf.
4 Souls United Not Of Skin.
4 Peace On Earth 2 Begin.

Whispers Of Eternal Bliss.
Prophecy, Is Heavens Kiss.
4 Worlds Of Joy & Of Fun.
4 Peace On Earth 2 Be Done.

Whispers Of Ancient Dreams,
4 Loyal Loves Silly Streams.
Angels Laughter Oh So, Clear.
4 Worlds Of Awe Joy & Cheer !

We Must 4-Give,
4 Our Soul 2 Live.
4 Ever More,
& Love 2 Endure.

4 Our Spirits Alive.
Links Of Love, 2 Thrive.
2 Eliminate, Neglect.
4 Love, 2 Protect.

Poverty Is Of Man.
Invest Yes U Can.
4 Missions, Galore,
& Peace 2 Endure.

Fund Joy & Empower.
4 Freedoms 2 Flower.
4 Choices 2 Arise,
Not Freedom, in Disguise.

2 Be Beacons, Of Light,
4 Kindness, In Flight.
2 Learn Peacemaking,
4 Loves, Awakening .

4 Honor As Worth,
& Heaven On Earth!

We R Women Of Mercy, 4 Empowering, Wit.
Taking Actions, 4 Worlds Of Love & Betterment.
As Our First Lady, Won't U Join Us, 4 Compassion ?
4 A Nation Of Freedom & Kindness, 2 Not Ration.

We R Women Of Peace, Striving 4 Freedom & Choices.
4 Worlds Of Awe & Wonder, 4 Loves Lost Voices.
In The Social Breeze Of Rules Gotten Out Of Hand.
Where Routes Exist Not 4 True Love, 2 Stand.

We Request Needs 4 Taxes Paid In Increments Of 5.
2 Keep The Powers Of Love In Action Vibrant & Alive.
We Are Women Asking 4 Our Elections, 2 Be Of Nice.
Where Peacemakers Meet Together 4 Loves, Slice.

We Are Women Not Out Do Harm, But Socially Empower.
Freedoms Rights, 2 Root, Bud Bloom & Flower.
As A First Lady May U Unite All, Even Past Elected.
4 A Secure Nation, Within 4 Honor That's Protected.

We Are Women Of America, Trying 2 Teach Others Right.
How 2 Use Our Words, 2 Become Beacons Of Light.
2 Honor Our Name United & The Rights Of Party Word Too.
With Visions Of Unity, 4 Peace On Earth, Pure & True.

Loyalty 2 Your Homeland Why Is It A Need ?
4 Your Peoples Roots 2 Prosper & Proceed.
4 Kinfolk, Neighbors, Friends Yet 2 Meet.
Tis Vital All Learn Honor & Respect, 2 Greet.

Loyalty 2 Unity 4 None, In Neglect Or Distress.
Loyalty 2 Love, 4 Paths Of Honors Success.
Loyalty 2 Freedoms Rights, 4 Loves Legacy.
Tis Vital All Learn That Honor Is A Good Key.

Loyalty 2 Your Homeland Why Bother At All ?
2 Answer The Call Of Duty 4 Love On Call.
Loyalty 2 Teaching Your Gov Right & All Around.
Tis A Need 4 Heaven On Earth Happy & Abound.

Loyalty 2 Humbleness, 4 Successes 2 Dock.
All Are Needed Traits 4 Merry Memories, 2 Lock.
Loyalty 2 Kindness 2 Neighbors & All, Afar.
Gives Birth 2 Heaven On Earths Twinkling Star !

In The Depths, Of A Teardrops, Gentle Flow.
One Can, Experience....Letting, Go.
In The Depths, Of A Teardrops, Lingering, Laugh.
One Can, Experience, A Humorous, Path.

In The Depths Of A Teardrop, Flowing, Free.
One Can Experience, A Inner, Purity.
In The Depths, Of A Teardrops, Gentle, Fall.
There's, Enough, Power, 2 Break Down, A Wall.

In The Depths, Of A Teardrops, Emotional, Ride.
Be Thankful, 4, The Tears, You've, Cried.
Be It , From Joy, Or Sorrow, Let, Them Flow.
4 The Inner, You, 2 Really Grow !

We Shall Rise Above, Hate & War.
4 Love In Action 2 Endure.
We Shall Rise Above, Discriminations.
4 A World Of Peace & Jubilations.

We Shall Rise, Above 4 Love, 2 Heal.
4 Heaven On Earth That's Surreal.
We Shall Rise Above, That I Know.
4 Love 2 Prosper Spread & Grow.

We Shall Rise Above & Get Along.
4 Peace On Earth 2 Grow Strong.
We Shall Rise Above, Bend Not Break.
4 Heaven On Earth In Our Wake .

In God's Light.

In God's Light.
There Is Sight.
In God's Rein.
There Is Gain.

In God's Care.
There Is Fair.
In Gods Instruction.
There Is Production.

In Gods Grace.
There's Every Race.
In Gods Season.
There Is Reason.

In Gods Living.
There Is Giving.
In Gods Root.
There Is Fruit.

In Gods Story.
There Is Glory.
In Gods Conception.
There Is Protection.

In Gods Birth.
There Is Worth.
In Gods Trinity.
There Is Infinity.

In Gods Gleaming.
There Is Meaning.
In Gods Evolution.
There Is Resolution.

In Gods Inspiration.
There Is Jubilation !

We The People Power, 4 Freedoms 2 Thrive.
Keeping The Forces, Of Pure Love Alive.
4 All 2 Partake, In Fruits Of Freedoms Rights.
4 Worlds Of Awe & Social Delights.

We The People Power, Shall Act 2 Uplift.
The Pursuits Of Happiness Not Set Adrift.
We The People Power, Shall Invest & Believe.
In Freedoms Rights, 4 Success, 2 Achieve.

In We The People Power, Here 2 Thrive Now.
4 All 2 Be Treated, As A Welcoming Wow.
We The People Power, Tired Of The Bickering.
4 Goals Of Peace On Earth, Alive & Flickering.

4 All Paths 2 Achieve, Happy Honors Success.
4 Freedom Of Choices 2 Awaken, 4 Progress.
In We The People Power , 4 Worlds Of Delight.
4 Freedom Of Choices, In Active Daily Flight.

We The People Power, 4 Joyous Love, Alive.
4 Peace On Earth, 2 Bud, Bloom & Thrive.

www.ingramcontent.com/pod-product-compliance
Lightning Source LLC
Chambersburg PA
CBHW060413080526
44583CB00012B/559